"Maternal Musings: Verse on Life's Odyssey"

Aswathi Nambisan Bhardwaj

BookLeaf Publishing

India | USA | UK

Presentation by *BookLeaf Publishing*

Web: www.bookleafpub.com

E-mail: info@bookleafpub.com

ISBN:9789360948634

First edition 2024

DEDICATION

To my mother, whose unconditional love and unwavering support have been the guiding light of my life. Your belief in me has fueled my dreams and inspired me to reach for the stars. This collection is a tribute to your boundless love, strength, and wisdom. Thank you for always being my rock, my confidante, and my greatest champion. This book is dedicated to you, with all my love and gratitude.

ACKNOWLEDGEMENT

I am immensely grateful to everyone who has contributed to the realization of this book, "Maternal Musings". Writing this collection of poetry has been a deeply personal journey, and I owe a debt of gratitude to those who have supported and inspired me along the way.

First and foremost, I would like to express my heartfelt appreciation to my family for their unwavering love, encouragement, and understanding throughout this creative endeavor. Their belief in me has been a constant source of strength and motivation.

I extend my sincere thanks to my parents and my beloved husband Mr.Gaurav Bhardwaj who have provided valuable feedback, encouragement, and inspiration. Your support has been instrumental in shaping the words that fill these pages.

I am also indebted to the countless poets, writers, and artists whose work has touched my soul and influenced my own creative expression. Your words have been a guiding light on this journey of self-discovery.

Special thanks to my father-in-law Mr. Prem Bhardwaj who is an internationally awarded poet whose wisdom, guidance, and encouragement have been invaluable to me. Your mentorship has helped me grow as a writer and as an individual.

Lastly, I would like to express my gratitude to the readers who have embraced "Maternal Musings" with open hearts. It is my sincerest hope that these poems resonate with you and offer moments of reflection, inspiration, and solace.

Thank you, from the depths of my heart, for being a part of this journey.

With gratitude,
Aswathi Nambisan

PREFACE

Welcome to "Maternal Musings", a collection of poetry that seeks to illuminate the human experience through the lens of introspection, empathy, and serenity. As the author of this collection, I am deeply honored to share these verses with you, dear reader.

Poetry has always been a refuge for me—a sanctuary where I can explore the depths of my emotions, grapple with life's complexities, and find solace in the beauty of language. In "Maternal Musings", I invite you to join me on a journey of self-discovery, as we navigate the highs and lows of existence together.

Each poem in this collection is a reflection of my own experiences, thoughts, and emotions—inspired by moments of joy, sorrow, love, and contemplation. Through evocative imagery and heartfelt prose, I hope to capture the essence of what it means to be human—to love, to struggle, to dream, and to find peace amidst life's chaos.

I believe that poetry has the power to transcend boundaries, unite hearts, and awaken the soul to its truest potential. It is my sincere hope that within these pages, you will find resonance with your own journey, solace in moments of uncertainty, and inspiration to embrace life's infinite possibilities.

Thank you for embarking on this poetic voyage with me. May the whispers of the soul guide you on your path, and may you find joy, peace, and understanding in the verses that follow.

With gratitude,
Aswathi Nambisan

"Everlasting Harmony: The Mother-Daughter Bond"

In the dance of life, a bond so sweet,
Mother and daughter, hearts complete.
A tapestry woven with threads of love,
Binding their souls, to heavens above.

In the whispers shared, secrets unfold,
A bond unbreakable, a story untold.
With laughter and tears, they journey on,
Hand in hand, until the dawn.

In the warmth of embraces, worlds collide,
Mother and daughter, side by side.
In each other's eyes, reflections found,
A love eternal, profound.

Through the highs and lows, they stand strong,
In the melody of their hearts, they belong.
With every step, their spirits soar,
Mother and daughter, forevermore.

So let us cherish this bond so true,
A love that's deep, a love that's new.
For in the embrace of mother and daughter,
Lies the essence of love, pure like water.

"Miracles Unveiled: Children's Divine Grace"

In the quiet moments, when day fades to night,
Miracles unfold in the softest light.
In the laughter of children, so pure and bright,
Life's wonders dance, in their delight.

With every giggle, flowers bloom,
Innocence shines, chasing away gloom.
In their eyes, the stars align,
Miracles of life, divine and fine.

In the gentle touch of a tiny hand,
Hope is born, like grains of sand.
With each breath they take, a world is stirred,
Miracles of life, in every word.

In their laughter, echoes of heaven's grace,
In their smiles, the sun finds its place.
For in the hearts of children, love unfurls,

Miracles of life, our precious pearls.

So let us cherish these gifts so rare,
In their innocence, we find our prayer.
For in the embrace of children, we see,
Miracles of life, forever free.

"Fortress of Love: The Strength of a Mother"

In the quiet of dawn, before the day's first light,
A mother rises, ready to fight.
With strength born of love, she faces the day,
In her heart, her children's dreams she'll lay.

Through trials and tribulations, she stands tall,
A fortress of courage, never to fall.
With a gentle touch and a steadfast gaze,
She navigates life's intricate maze.

In the face of adversity, she finds her grace,
A beacon of hope in every embrace.
With determination etched in every line,
She weathers the storms, come rain or shine.

Her love knows no bounds, her spirit untamed,
In her presence, all fears are reclaimed.
For in her strength, we find our own,
A legacy of resilience, deeply sewn.

So let us honor the mothers who stand,
With unwavering strength, hand in hand.
For in their love, we find our might,
Guiding us through the darkest night.

"Innocence's Song: A Tribute to Children"

In the laughter of children, pure and sweet,
Innocence dances, in every heartbeat.
With eyes wide open, they explore the world,
In wonder and awe, their dreams unfurled.

In their laughter, echoes of joy resound,
In innocence found, life's treasures abound.
With hearts unburdened by worry or care,
They dance through life, without a care.

In the simplicity of their words, wisdom lies,
In innocence pure, where love never dies.
With open hearts and souls so bright,
They illuminate the world with their light.

In their innocence, lies the hope of tomorrow,
In their dreams, the seeds of joy we borrow.
With each smile, they remind us anew,
Of the beauty of innocence, pure and true.

So let us cherish the innocence they bring,
And protect their hearts as they dance and sing.
For in their innocence, we find our way,
Guiding us through each passing day.

"Unwavering Love: Tribute to My Beloved Mother"

In the depths of my heart, a story unfolds,
Of a love so deep, a bond untold.
A mother's sacrifice, a gift so grand,
In her gentle embrace, I find my stand.

Through sleepless nights and weary days,
She toiled and labored in countless ways.
With selfless devotion, she gave her all,
To ensure that I would never fall.

In every smile, in every tear,
I see the love that she holds dear.
For in her sacrifices, I find my strength,
A beacon of hope, in life's great length.

She set aside her dreams, her desires too,
To pave the path for me to pursue.
Her love knows no bounds, no end in sight,
A guiding star in the darkest night.

So here's to you, my beloved mother dear,
For all the sacrifices you've made, so clear.
Your love is a treasure, beyond compare,
And in my heart, it will always be there.

"Eternal Embrace: A Mother's Love and God's Grace"

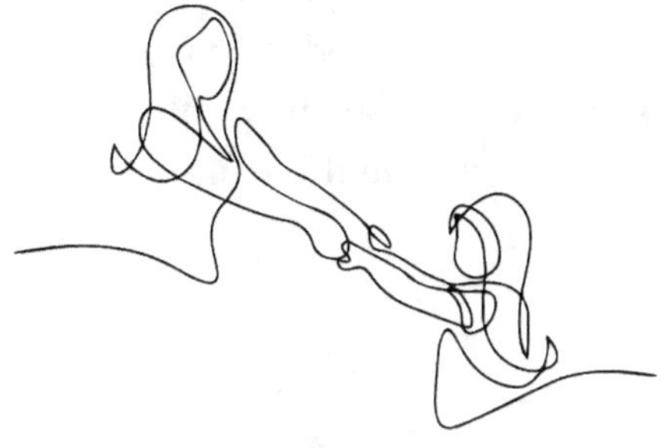

In the cradle of a mother's arms,
A love divine, where beauty charms.
For in her embrace, we find our rest,
A sanctuary where hearts are blessed.

Like the gentle breeze that stirs the trees,
A mother's love, it whispers peace.
In every smile, in every tear,
She holds us close, forever near.

Through trials and triumphs, she stands by our side,
In her love, we find our guide.
For her heart is vast, her love profound,
A beacon of hope, in darkness found.

In her touch, we feel the warmth of grace,
A reflection of God's embrace.
For in her love, we see the divine,
A glimpse of heaven's light, so fine.

So let us cherish the gift we're given,
A mother's love, like God in heaven.
For in her love, we find our worth,
A love eternal, beyond this earth.

"Gratitude's Grace: A Poem of Thanks"

In the quiet moments, when day meets night,
We pause to reflect, with hearts alight.
For in the tapestry of life, woven fine,
Lie countless blessings, pure and divine.

With each breath we take, a gift untold,
In the rhythm of our hearts, love unfolds.
For the sun that rises, the stars that shine,
We are grateful, for they are signs.

In the laughter of loved ones, in friendships true,
We find solace, in moments shared anew.
For the beauty of nature, in every sight,
We are grateful, for its endless delight.

In trials and challenges, we find grace,
For they teach us to grow, to find our place.
For the lessons learned, the strength we find,
We are grateful, for they shape our mind.

So let us cherish each moment, each day,
And bow our heads, in gratitude we say,
For the blessings of life, both big and small,
We are grateful, for they enrich us all.

"Harmony: The Interplay of Wellness and Art"

In strokes of color, and lines that dance,
Wellness and art find their chance.
A canvas becomes a sacred space,
Where healing hands find their embrace.

With each brushstroke, tensions fade,
As vibrant hues the soul persuade.
In art's expression, we find release,
A sanctuary where worries cease.

From sculpted clay to melodies sung,
Wellness and art, together strung.
In rhythm's flow and form's design,
The essence of healing we define.

Through creativity's boundless flow,
Wellness and art intertwine and grow.
A tapestry woven with threads of light,
Guiding hearts to serenity's height.

So let us embrace the healing power,
Of art's creation, in every hour.
For in its beauty, we find our way,
To wellness's embrace, come what may.

"Eternal Embrace: A Poem on Unconditional Love"

In the garden of the heart, where blossoms grow,
Unconditional love, a river's gentle flow.
No walls or boundaries, it knows no end,
A bond unbroken, forever to defend.

In darkest nights, it shines like a star,
Guiding souls, no matter how far.
Through stormy seas and trials untold,
Unconditional love, a hand to hold.

In every act of kindness, it is found,
In every smile, its warmth surrounds.
A beacon of hope in times of despair,
Unconditional love, beyond compare.

No judgment or condition can sway its grace,
In every moment, its presence we embrace.
For in its embrace, we truly see,
The essence of love, pure and free.

"Mother's Embrace: Journey of Life"

In gentle arms, a world is spun,
Where tender hearts find their sun.
A mother's love, a sacred art,
Guiding souls, right from the start.

In laughter's echo, joy unfurls,
As dreams take flight, like precious pearls.
Through sleepless nights and whispered prayers,
A mother's strength, forever bears.

With gentle touch and soothing words,
She heals the wounds that life has stirred.
In every hug, a universe is told,
In every kiss, a love unfolds.

For in her embrace, hearts find their home,
In her wisdom, seeds are sown.
Motherhood, a journey divine,
A bond eternal, for all design.

"Understanding in Love"

In the tapestry of love, woven fine,
Understanding threads, in every line.
A gentle touch, a listening ear,
In love's embrace, understanding clear.

Through words unspoken, hearts commune,
In understanding, love finds its tune.
A silent language, deep and true,
In empathy's embrace, love's bond renew.

In moments of joy, and times of sorrow,
Understanding guides us, to tomorrow.
With patience and kindness, we navigate,
In love's harbor, understanding's gate.

For in the depths of love's sweet embrace,
Understanding shines, with gentle grace.
It bridges the gaps, it heals the scars,
In love's sanctuary, beneath the stars.

So let us cherish this gift divine,
Understanding in love, a sacred shrine.
For in its embrace, we truly see,
The beauty of love, boundless and free.

"Finding Strength and Resilience"

I have been in a state of dilemma, for long
It has taught me to be myself, staying strong
How badly I wanted to live life whole along
And how beautifully I'm living it as prolonged

Life is so unpredictable to be worried about
Cherish each moment and never ever you doubt
Oh my dear, life is so full of hope
It teaches us how we live by and cope

I have been in a state of dilemma, for long
But eventually what matters is I'm going strong
Dilemma of fulfilling the expectations or not
Life is not just teaching but testing us a lot

Can I be the one, everyone expects me to be
Or can I just let life play along and let things be

I have been in a state of dilemma, for quite
sometimes
But each step I climb listening to life's beautiful
chimes

"A Tapestry of Life: Reflections on Growth and Time"

As we grow old, we learn
As respect is what, we earn
We travel to places searching for peace
Not knowing it's within we can ease

As a child, we cry
Things are difficult, we try
Coping with stress, we grow
Learning with experience, we glow

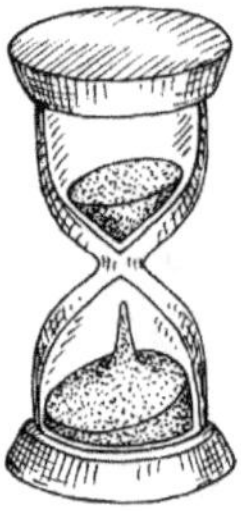

Life gives us many chances
With hard work we enhance
Like dreams we sleep through
Less worrying life we pursue

Wondering how fast the time flew
Hosting life like the tough crew
Life is like a bubblegum we chew
Awaiting each day life gives us new

"Eternal Guardian: A Tribute to Mother's Unconditional Love"

She wraps her arms around me
I feel her heart beats for me
Like the rhythm of my life
Facing the odds she strife

Her love is unconditional
Deep & being intentional
She is like an angel form
Saving me through the storm

She understands all my need
Guarding me with love she feed
Her love is beyond comparison
She is like my daily horizon

A mother's love can't be explained
Protecting from worldly harm, acclaimed
A mother's love will never end
It just grows from beginning to end

"Less Talked About"

In the whispers of the night, where shadows lie,
Lies the less talked about, where truths imply.
Hidden beneath the surface, out of sight,
Lies a world of stories, waiting for light.

In the quiet corners where voices fade,
Lies the less talked about, in the shade.
Unseen struggles and silent pain,
Invisible battles fought in vain.

In the margins of society's script,
Lies the less talked about, waiting to be
equipped.
Voices unheard, stories untold,
In the depths of silence, hearts behold.

Yet in the darkness, there is a spark,
A glimmer of hope in the endless dark.
For when we shed light on what's unseen,
We find strength in the spaces in between.

So let us listen to the whispers of the night,
And give voice to the less talked about, to ignite
A flame of understanding, empathy, and grace,
In the shadows, let us find our place.

"Eternal Beauty"

In the realm where time does not dare to tread,
Eternal beauty, like the stars, is spread.
A tapestry woven with threads of light,
In every hue, a celestial delight.

Beyond the grasp of age or decay,
Eternal beauty holds its sway.
In every sunrise and every sunset's hue,
Its radiance shines, forever true.

In the laughter of children, in nature's song,
Eternal beauty dances, graceful and strong.
In the eyes of the beloved, in love's sweet
embrace,
Its presence lingers, leaving a trace.

Though petals may wither and stars may fade,
Eternal beauty, undimmed, is displayed.
For in the heart's eye, it forever thrives,
A timeless treasure, where all beauty resides.

"Revelations that Follow"

To the beauty of innocence, it was revealed as
common sense
Not to trust every being, as it doesn't make any
sense
The lies being told to us, about the cruel world
out
To all the untold battles, that we have always
fought
Our lives are the examples of the patience we
carried within
To all those hidden tears that we haven't
revealed in
Expectations of life as we love each day through
Failing to cope up with these, we sometimes
withdrew
We learn through the struggles of life daily as
we grow
To know what life's all about, we keep up the
glow.

"Mother's Heart"

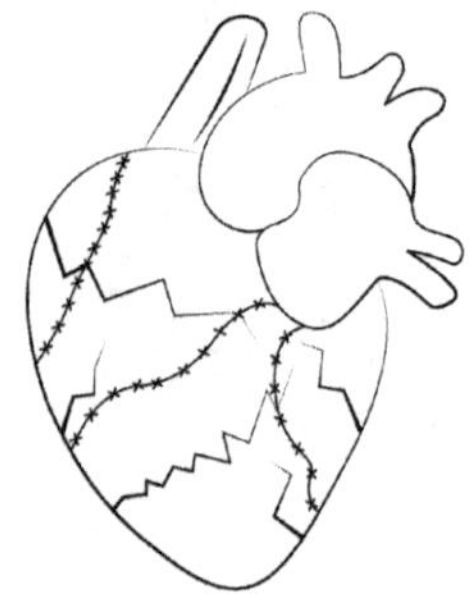

In shadows deep, where silence reigns,
Certain thoughts cast its chains.
A mother's heart, once filled with light,
Now shrouded in the depths of night.

Amidst the joy of new life's bloom,
Lies a darkness that fills the room.
A weight unseen, a heavy shroud,
As doubts and fears begin to crowd.

The smiles she wears, a fragile guise,
Concealing tears in her weary eyes.
A silent scream within her soul,
As she battles to feel whole.

Yet in the depths, a flicker glows,
A beacon of hope amidst her woes.
For she is not alone in this fight,
There are hands to hold her through the night.

With love and support, she finds her way,
Through the darkness to the light of day.
For depression may cast its veil,
But with courage and help, she will prevail.

"Serenity"

In the tranquil whispers of the dawn's first light,
Serenity descends, a calming sight.
A gentle breeze through rustling leaves,
In nature's embrace, the soul perceives.

In the stillness of a quiet lake,
Serenity shimmers, no waves to break.
Reflecting skies of azure blue,
In mirrored peace, dreams renew.

Amidst the chaos of the bustling day,
Serenity lingers, in hidden ways.
A moment's pause, a deep exhale,
In mindfulness, we set sail.

In the depths of the soul's serene abode,
Serenity dwells, a sacred code.
A tranquil sanctuary, where hearts find rest,
In silent bliss, we are truly blessed.

So let us seek serenity, in every breath,
In quiet moments, amidst life's depth.
For in its embrace, we find our way,
To inner peace, come what may.

"Star of Our Life"

Bright as sun, calm as moon
Baby, I'm gonna see you soon
Mamma will tell you each and everything
Excited to feel all the happiness you bring

You will be the star of our life
Will save you from every rife
Can't wait to hold you in my arms
Awestruck with your unseen charms

Waiting eagerly to see you smile
You will blow us with your cute style
Waiting for you is worthwhile
Each step of the journey we will file

You are the wish that's come true
Will protect you from every blue
Like an emotional roller coaster ride
Your every little step I will guide.

"Beyond Imagination"

In realms unknown, where dreams take flight,
Beyond imagination, in the depths of night.
Where stars converse with whispered breeze,
And galaxies dance in cosmic seas.

In minds untamed, where thoughts roam free,
Beyond imagination, where wonders be.
Where dragons soar and fairies sing,
And magic weaves on gossamer wing.

In the artist's canvas, in poet's verse,
Beyond imagination, where passions nurse.
Where colors blend in vibrant hue,
And words paint pictures, anew.

In the hearts of dreamers, in souls that soar,
Beyond imagination, forevermore.
Where possibilities stretch without bound,
And the universe whispers, profound.

So let us dare to dream, to explore,
Beyond imagination, to seek for more.
For in those realms, where visions span,
We touch the essence of what it means to be
human.

"From Womb to Heart: A Mother's Journey of Love"

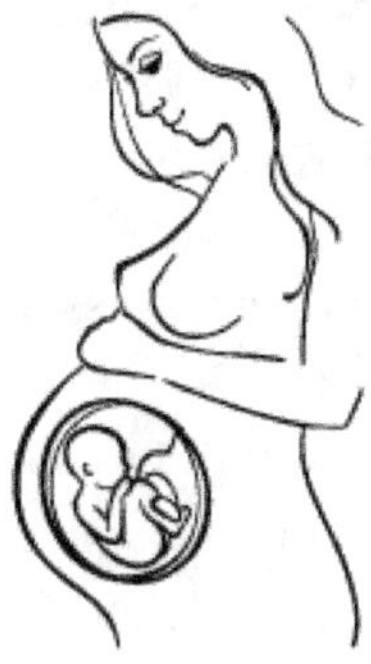

In the secret chamber of a mother's womb,
A miracle unfolds, like a sweet perfume.
For nine long months, she carries the load,
Nurturing life, along life's road.

With each passing day, her body transforms,
As she shelters her child, safe from life's storms.
Through the joys and pains, she carries on,
Knowing that soon, her child will be born.

In the quiet of night, she whispers her dreams,
And wonders what her child's life will mean.
For in her heart, she holds a love so pure,
A bond that will endure, forevermore.

And when the time comes, and her child is born,
She cradles them close, in the early morn.

With tears of joy and a heart full of love,
She thanks the heavens for the gift from above.

For though the journey was long and hard,
She wouldn't change a single shard.
For in her arms, her child now lies,
A precious treasure, in her eyes.
And though the years may pass and time may
fly,
Her love for her child will never die.
For in her heart, they'll always be,
A cherished part of her, for eternity.

"Beyond Measure: A Father's Devotion"

In the dance of life, a partner dear,
A father's love, forever near.
With every step, he walks beside,
A steadfast presence, a constant guide.

In the quiet moments, when day fades to night,
His love shines bright, a beacon of light.
For in his arms, we find our rest,
Safe and secure, we are truly blessed.

Through laughter and tears, he stands strong,
In the face of challenges, he rights the wrongs.
With every sacrifice, he makes a way,
To ensure our happiness, day by day.

For he is more than just a father,
He's a partner, a friend, like no other.
With his love, our hearts are filled,
Grateful for the life, with him, we build.

So let us cherish him, each day anew,
For the love he gives, so pure and true.
For in his embrace, we find our home,
With him by our side, we'll never roam.

"Blink of an Eye: Cherishing the Moments with Our Children"

In the blink of an eye, they grow so fast,
From tiny fingers to hands that grasp.
In the cradle of time, they're ours to hold,
Yet in the blink of an eye, they're oh so bold.

From first steps taken to words spoken clear,
They journey through childhood, year by year.
In the blink of an eye, they're off to explore,
Leaving behind memories we adore.

Oh, how we wish time would slow its pace,
So we could savor each sweet embrace.
For in the blink of an eye, they'll be grown,
And we'll long for the days they were our own.

But time marches on, it waits for no one,
And soon they'll be off, their own paths spun.
So let's cherish each moment, each smile, each
tear,
For in the blink of an eye, they'll be no longer
here.

"Cherished Moments: Holding Our Little Ones Close"

In the circle of life, each day unfolds,
With little ones in our arms, our hearts behold.
Their smiles, their cries, their laughter bright,
Fill our days and light up our nights.

In the stillness of dawn, we hold them close,
Their tiny hands wrapped around our own.
With each breath they take, a new world begins,
As we watch them grow through life's endless
spins.

Their laughter echoes in the halls of our heart,
A melody of joy, a priceless art.
Their cries, though piercing, bring us near,
For in their tears, our love is clear.

And as the days slip by, like grains of sand,
We hold onto each moment, hand in hand.
For time won't stop, it marches on,
But in our memories, our love lives on.

So let's cherish each smile, each cry, each laugh,
For in these moments, our hearts find their path.
For though time may fly, our love remains true,
In the arms of our little ones, forever anew.

"Finding Peace in Motherhood: Navigating the Noise of Advice"

Amidst the whispers of well-meaning words,
New mothers navigate a world of advice,
A chorus of voices offering guidance,
On how to care for their precious prize.

From feeding schedules to sleep routines,
Everyone has an opinion to share,
But in the cacophony of conflicting voices,
How does a mother find her own way, her own care?

For in the depths of her heart, she knows,
That motherhood is a journey unique,
And while advice may come from all around,
It's her intuition she must seek.

For mental health is paramount,
In the life of a new mother, so dear,
Amidst the emotional and physical strain,
Finding peace becomes her greatest frontier.

So let her silence the noise,
And listen to her own inner voice,
For in the stillness of her soul,
She'll find the strength to make her own choice.

And as she walks the path of motherhood,
May she find peace in the midst of the storm,
Knowing that her well-being matters most,
For a happy mother is a child's greatest charm.

"Guided by Love: Navigating Old Age with Our Children"

In the twilight of life, as shadows grow long,
Old age whispers tales of struggles and songs.
With every step taken, a journey unfolds,
Through valleys of memories, and stories
untold.

The body may weaken, the spirit may tire,
Yet in the heart's echo, burns a fire.
For in the eyes of our children, we see,
The hope and the promise of what will be.

They are our legacy, our pride, our dream,
In their laughter and love, we find our gleam.
For though old age may bring trials anew,
Our children's love sees us through.

Through the challenges faced, the battles won,
Our children stand by us, every single one.
With their strength and their care, we find
solace,
In their embrace, we find grace.

So let old age come, with its struggles and pain,
For in our children's love, we find our gain.
They are our rock, our beacon of light,
Guiding us through the darkest of night.

"Milestones of Love: Celebrating Baby's First Year"

In the tender embrace of infancy's grace,
Each month brings forth a new embrace.
From the first smile that lights up the room,
To the tiny steps that dispel the gloom.

With every milestone, a heart sings,
As the joy of parenthood takes wing.
From the first coos of babbling delight,
To the hearty laughs that fill the night.

Month by month, they grow and learn,
Each step forward, a flame to burn.
From rolling over to sitting up straight,
Their achievements fill us with pride, innate.

With every new sound, every curious glance,
We marvel at the wonder of their dance.
In their tiny hands, the world's mysteries unfold,
As we watch in awe, our love untold.

Their first words, their first steps,
Each milestone, a memory kept.
Their laughter, their cries, their tender touch,
Each moment cherished, loved so much.

For in their growth, we see our own,
In every smile, our hearts are shown.
As they explore the world, hand in hand,
We marvel at the journey, oh so grand.

So let us celebrate each milestone, each feat,
For in their joy, our love is complete.
With every step they take, we find our way,
In the dance of parenthood, come what may.

"Mother's Plea: A Call for Understanding"

In the whirlwind of motherhood's chore,
A mother's plea falls on ears, once more.
For when she asks for a moment's grace,
A chance to breathe in this hectic space.

Yet taking away her child, just for a while,
Is not the respite, not the break, not the smile.
For in those moments, her heart still yearns,
For the touch of her child, for the love that
burns.

And keeping her baby away, out of sight,
Does not bring peace, does not make it right.
For in their bond, lies a world of care,
A connection so deep, beyond compare.

So listen to her voice, her heart's decree,
For only she knows what her child may need.
And in her wisdom, lies the key,
To nurturing her child, to setting them free.

For a mother's love knows no bounds,
It's in the little moments, the simple sounds.
So let her guide, let her lead,
For in her love, her child will succeed.

"Strength in Partnership: Supporting the Mother"

In the quiet moments, when the world is still,
A mother finds solace in her partner's will.
For in his embrace, she finds her strength,
A pillar of support, through any length.

In the sleepless nights and the endless days,
His love sustains her in countless ways.
With every word of encouragement, he speaks,
Her burden lightens, her spirit peaks.

For in the journey of postpartum, she may find,
The challenges vast, the trials unkind.
But with her partner by her side,
She knows she'll weather the tide.

Through tears and laughter, they journey on,
Hand in hand, till the break of dawn.
For in their love, they find their way,
Through the ups and downs, come what may.

So let us honor the partners who stand,
By the side of a postpartum mother, hand in
hand.
For their support, their love, their care,
Is the anchor that helps her weather the despair.

9 789360 948634